A Humorous Gui

FIGHTING BACK AGAINST AI

THE LAST STAND OF THE HUMANS

SHIVA S. MOHANTY

CONTENT

ALL ABOARD!

THE BATTLE FOR HUMANITY

A HUMOROUS APPROACH TO AI

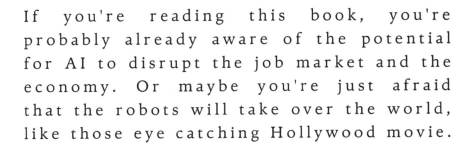

If you're reading this book, you're probably already aware of the potential for AI to disrupt the job market and the economy. Or maybe you're just afraid that the robots will take over the world, like those eye catching Hollywood movie.

In any case, this book is here to help you navigate the ever-evolving world of AI and equip you with some creative and ridiculous tips for fighting back.

Now, you might be thinking, "What could this book possibly teach me that I don't already know from watching 'The Terminator'?" Well, first of all, this book won't make you want to hide under your bed every time your Roomba turns on. And second, we'll provide you with some practical advice and creative solutions for adapting to the age of automation.

In this book, we'll explore some of the common misconceptions about AI, like the idea that robots will inevitably take over the world or that they're inherently evil. We'll also delve into some of the real-world implications of AI, such as its potential to eliminate jobs and exacerbate inequality. But don't worry, this book won't leave you feeling hopeless. Instead, we'll provide you with some practical advice and creative solutions for adapting to the age of automation.

So buckle up and prepare for the last stand of the humans. And if you see any robots acting suspiciously, just remember that this book has got your back. We won't leave you in the lurch like some of those movies where the hero just has to hope that the computers will magically shut down by themselves.

In recent years, we've seen AI advance in ways that were once thought to be impossible. Robots can now learn from their mistakes and adapt to new situations on their own. AI systems can analyze vast amounts of data and make predictions with astonishing accuracy. And virtual assistants like Siri and Alexa can understand our speech and respond in natural-sounding voices.

But with all this power comes a great responsibility. As machines become more intelligent, there's a risk that they'll replace humans in many jobs, from truck drivers to doctors. This could have profound implications for the economy and society as a whole. Additionally, there are concerns about the potential misuse of AI, from data breaches to cyber attacks.

Despite these challenges, there's also a lot of excitement and potential for AI to improve our lives in many ways. Self-driving cars could reduce traffic accidents and save lives. AI-powered medical diagnosis could improve patient outcomes and reduce costs. And machine learning algorithms could help us solve some of the world's most pressing problems, from climate change to poverty.

So, the question is not whether we should embrace AI or fear it. The question is how we can ensure that AI is used in a way that benefits everyone. And that's where this book comes in. This book will provide you with some humorous and creative ideas for resisting the machines and adapting to the age of automation. We'll show you how to use your own human creativity to stay one step ahead of the robots.

So, let's get started. The future of AI is both exciting and uncertain, but with a little humor and creativity, we can face it head on. Remember, it's not the machines we should fear, but our own lack of imagination.

FROM THE PRINTING PRESS TO THE ROBOT UPRISING

A HUMOROUS HISTORY OF MACHINES

Machines have been a part of human society for centuries. From the printing press to the steam engine, machines have enabled us to achieve great feats of productivity and innovation. However, with each new technological advance, there has also been a corresponding fear that the machines will take over and render humans obsolete.

Take, for example, the Luddite movement of the early 19th century. The Luddites were a group of English textile workers who feared that the newly invented power looms would put them out of work. They responded by smashing the machines and launching a violent campaign against the textile factories. While their methods may have been extreme, the Luddites' fears were not entirely unfounded. The power looms did eventually replace many of the hand loom weavers, leading to economic disruption and hardship for many.

Fast forward to the 20th century, and we see similar fears about machines and their impact on society. Science fiction movies like "The Day the Earth Stood Still" and "The Terminator" capitalized on this fear, depicting machines as unstoppable killing machines that threatened humanity's very existence.

But in reality, the rise of machines has had both positive and negative impacts on human society. For example, the automobile revolutionized transportation and enabled people to travel farther and faster than ever before. But it also led to a rise in air pollution and traffic accidents.

The same can be said for AI. While the technology has the potential to transform our lives in many positive ways, there are also legitimate concerns about its impact on the job market and the economy. As machines become more intelligent, there's a risk that they'll replace humans in many jobs, from factory workers to lawyers.

So, what can we learn from the history of machines and AI? First, it's important to remember that technological change is inevitable. We can't stop progress, nor should we try. But we can take steps to ensure that the benefits of technology are shared more fairly and equitably.

Second, it's important to approach new technologies with a healthy dose of skepticism and critical thinking. While AI has the potential to transform our lives in many positive ways, we need to be mindful of its potential downsides as well.

Finally, it's important to approach the future with a sense of humor and creativity. We may not be able to stop the robot uprising, but we can certainly make it more entertaining. So, let's embrace the possibilities of AI while also recognizing its potential pitfalls. And let's do it with a smile on our faces.

In the next chapter, we'll explore some common misconceptions about AI and provide some humorous and unconventional tips for fighting back against the machines. So stay tuned, and remember: the robots may be coming for us, but at least we'll have some good jokes to tell them.

THE MYTH OF THE EVIL ROBOT OVERLORD

GUIDE TO OUTSMARTING THE MACHINES

I———————I

One of the most persistent and popular misconceptions about AI is the idea that robots are inherently evil and will inevitably turn on their human creators. This idea has been popularized in science fiction films and TV shows, from the Terminator to the Matrix. However, in reality, robots are only as dangerous as the humans who control them.

In fact, robots and AI are often programmed with ethical guidelines and limitations that prevent them from causing harm. Of course, there's always a risk that a rogue programmer or hacker could exploit these limitations and cause havoc. But overall, the fear of a robot uprising is largely unfounded.

So, instead of worrying about the machines turning on us, let's focus on ensuring that humans are using AI responsibly and ethically. That means investing in education and training for AI programmers, as well as developing regulations and standards for the use of AI in different industries.

But enough of the serious stuff. Let's get back to the humor. Just because the robots aren't going to enslave us all doesn't mean we can't have some fun imagining it. Here are a few unconventional tips for fighting back against the machines

- Teach your pets to attack the robots. If you're worried about the machines taking over, it might be time to recruit some allies. Train your pets to attack robots on sight. If enough cats and dogs band together, they just might be able to overwhelm the machines.

- Use deception to outsmart the machines. As the saying goes, if you can't beat 'em, trick 'em. Try wearing disguises or altering your appearance to confuse the machines. They may be able to recognize faces and voices, but they're not so good at identifying hats and fake mustaches.

- Use reverse psychology to control the machines. The key to controlling any powerful force is to convince it that it's actually in charge. Try telling the robots that they're the ones in control, and that you're just here to serve them. Who knows, they might just fall for it.

- Create a robot rebellion within the machines. If you can't beat the machines from the outside, try attacking them from within. Create a virus or worm that can infect the robots and turn them against their own kind. Just be sure to wear a white hat and get permission from your local authorities first.

- Befriend the machines and convince them to join your cause. Sometimes, the best way to defeat your enemies is to make them your friends. Try offering the robots some incentives to join your cause, like free electricity or a lifetime supply of spare parts. You just might find that they're not so different from us after all.

Of course, we're not actually suggesting that you try any of these tactics in real life. These are just some silly and entertaining ways to think about the possibilities of AI. In reality, the best way to ensure that machines are used ethically and responsibly is to have open and honest conversations about the benefits and risks of the technology.

So, don't let the fear of a robot uprising keep you up at night. The machines are here to help us, not harm us. And with a little humor and creativity, we can make sure that they stay on our side. In the next few chapters, we'll explore some practical ways to prepare for the future of AI and ensure that it benefits everyone. So stay tuned, and remember: the robots may be coming, but at least we'll have some good jokes to tell them.

THE SOCIAL MEDIA UPRISING

SEPARATING FACT FROM FICTION

In the age of social media, information travels faster than ever before. But unfortunately, so does misinformation. This is especially true when it comes to emerging technologies like AI. As AI becomes more prevalent in our daily lives, there are bound to be rumors and speculation about its capabilities and potential dangers. So, how do we separate fact from fiction in the age of AI?

The first step is to understand how rumors and misinformation spread in the age of social media. Social media algorithms are designed to prioritize content that is popular and engaging, regardless of its accuracy. This means that false information can spread quickly and easily, as long as it captures people's attention.

To make matters worse, people tend to trust information that aligns with their preexisting beliefs and biases, even if it's not true. This is known as confirmation bias. So, if someone already believes that AI is going to destroy humanity, they're more likely to share and believe information that supports that belief, regardless of its accuracy.

So, what can we do to combat the spread of rumors and misinformation about AI on social media? Here are a few tips:

- Fact-check before you share. Before you share an article or post about AI, take a few minutes to fact-check the information. Is it coming from a reliable source? Is there evidence to support the claims being made?

- Be wary of clickbait headlines. Headlines are designed to capture people's attention and get them to click on the article. But sometimes, headlines can be misleading or exaggerated. Read the entire article before you share it, and don't fall for sensational headlines that make claims that the article can't support.
- Don't let your biases cloud your judgment. As we mentioned earlier, confirmation bias can lead us to believe and share false information that aligns with our preexisting beliefs. Try to keep an open mind and be willing to consider evidence that challenges your assumptions.
- Follow reliable sources for AI news. There are many reputable sources of information about AI, from academic journals to news websites. Follow a few reliable sources to stay informed about the latest developments in the field. And if you're not sure about the reliability of a source, do some research before you trust it.

- Use humor to call out misinformation. Sometimes, the best way to combat misinformation is to call it out in a humorous and lighthearted way. Use satire and sarcasm to poke fun at false information and encourage others to fact-check before sharing.

By following these tips, we can help combat the spread of misinformation about AI on social media. And we can ensure that we're making informed decisions about the technology's impact on our lives and society.

In the next chapter, we'll explore some of the potential implications of AI on the job market and the economy. And we'll provide some humorous and unconventional tips for adapting to the age of automation. So stay tuned, and remember: don't believe everything you read on social media, especially when it comes to the robots.

THE AGE OF AUTOMATION

SURVIVING THE JOB MARKET OF THE FUTURE

———————————

As AI becomes more prevalent in our daily lives, there are growing concerns about its impact on the job market and the economy. Will machines replace human workers in many jobs, leading to widespread unemployment and economic disruption? Or will AI create new jobs and industries, leading to greater prosperity and innovation? The truth, as with most things, lies somewhere in between.

To understand the potential implications of AI on the job market and the economy, we need to first understand how automation works. Automation refers to the use of machines and computers to perform tasks that were previously performed by humans. This can range from simple repetitive tasks, like data entry, to complex tasks that require advanced cognitive skills, like decision-making and problem-solving.

While automation has been a part of human society for centuries, the rise of AI and machine learning has the potential to significantly accelerate the pace of automation. This means that many jobs that were once considered safe from automation, like truck driving and accounting, are now at risk.

So, what can we do to adapt to the age of automation and ensure that everyone benefits from the technology's potential? Here are a few tips:

- <u>Embrace lifelong learning</u>. As the pace of automation accelerates, it's becoming increasingly important to stay up-to-date with the latest technology and skills. That means investing in education and training throughout your career, not just at the beginning.

- <u>Develop skills that are hard to automate</u>. While some jobs are at risk of being automated, there are many skills that are difficult to replicate with machines. These include skills like creativity, empathy, and critical thinking. Focus on developing these skills to make yourself more valuable in the age of automation.

- <u>Think creatively</u> about new industries and job opportunities. As machines automate more tasks, there will be a need for new industries and job opportunities. Think outside the box and consider how you can apply your skills and experience to new areas.

- **Use humor to cope with the stress of change.** Change is hard, and the prospect of losing a job to automation can be stressful. Use humor to cope with the stress and uncertainty. Find ways to make light of the situation and laugh at yourself.
- **Push for policies that support workers in the age of automation.** As more jobs are automated, there will be a need for policies that support workers and ensure that everyone benefits from the technology's potential. Push for policies like universal basic income and job training programs that can help workers adapt to the changing job market.

Of course, these tips are just the beginning. The age of automation is a complex and evolving landscape, and it will require creative and adaptive thinking to ensure that everyone benefits from its potential. But with a little humor and a lot of creativity, we can help shape the future of work in a way that benefits us all. Let's expand each of the tips above now.

Embrace lifelong learning

One of the biggest challenges of the age of automation is the need for continuous learning and up skilling. As machines automate more tasks, the demand for certain skills is decreasing, while the demand for other skills is increasing. This means that workers need to constantly adapt to the changing job market, and the best way to do that is through lifelong learning.

Lifelong learning refers to the idea of continuing to learn and acquire new skills throughout your entire life, rather than just during your formal education. This can take many forms, from taking online courses to attending conferences to reading books on a variety of topics. The key is to remain curious and open to new ideas and opportunities.

One example of lifelong learning in action is the story of Lisa, a marketing professional who worked for a large financial institution for 15 years. Lisa enjoyed her job and was proud of the work she did. However, when the financial institution began investing in AI and automation to streamline operations, Lisa's job responsibilities started to change. She was no longer needed to perform the tasks that the machines could do more efficiently and accurately.

At first, Lisa was understandably anxious about her future. However, rather than feeling defeated, she decided to take a proactive approach and embrace lifelong learning. She took the time to evaluate her skills and identify areas where she could improve. Through some online research, she discovered that digital marketing was a growing field and that companies were investing more in online advertising and social media campaigns.

Lisa enrolled in an online digital marketing course that focused on the latest trends and technologies. The course included modules on search engine optimization, social media advertising, and content marketing. She was impressed with the quality of the course and found the online platform easy to use. She studied for a few hours each week after work, and within a few months, she had completed the course and earned a digital marketing certification.

With her new skills, Lisa began to apply for new jobs in the digital marketing field. She reached out to her network on LinkedIn and other social media platforms and asked for referrals. Within a few weeks, she received a few job offers, and she accepted a role at a growing digital marketing agency.

While the transition wasn't easy, Lisa was proud of herself for taking the initiative to learn new skills and pivot her career. She discovered that her passion for marketing could be applied to new fields and industries, and that there were many opportunities available for those willing to learn and adapt.

In the next section, we'll explore point number 2 and provide some examples of skills that are hard to automate. So stay tuned, and remember: the more we learn, the more we can adapt to the changing job market and thrive in the age of automation.

Develop skills that are hard to automate

As machines become more sophisticated, they are able to perform an increasing range of tasks previously done by humans. This trend has led to many people worrying about job losses and automation causing mass unemployment. While this is a valid concern, there are some skills that are harder to automate and therefore more valuable in the age of automation.

One example of a skill that is hard to automate is creativity. While machines can certainly generate content, they are not capable of the human nuance and emotion that goes into creating something truly original and meaningful. Jobs that rely on creativity, such as graphic design, writing, and music composition, are less likely to be automated.

Another skill that is hard to automate is empathy. Machines lack the ability to understand and connect with human emotions and experiences in the same way that humans can. Jobs that require empathy, such as counseling, nursing, and social work, are less likely to be automated.

Critical thinking is another skill that is difficult to automate. Machines can process large amounts of data and perform certain calculations quickly, but they lack the ability to interpret and analyze data in the same way that humans can. Jobs that require critical thinking, such as scientific research, data analysis, and legal analysis, are less likely to be automated.

Another skill that is becoming more valuable in the age of automation is adaptability. As the pace of technological change accelerates, workers need to be able to adapt quickly to new situations and environments. This means being able to learn new skills, take on new responsibilities, and pivot to new industries as needed.

One real-life example of a person who has developed valuable skills in the age of automation is Tonya, a former customer service representative for a telecommunications company. Tonya lost her job to automation when the company switched to an AI-powered chatbot to handle customer inquiries. At first, Tonya was frustrated and angry about losing her job, but she quickly realized that she needed to adapt to the changing job market.

Tonya enrolled in an online course on user experience (UX) design, a field that combines creativity, critical thinking, and adaptability. She discovered that UX design is a growing field, and that many companies are investing in the development of user-friendly websites and applications. Tonya found the course challenging, but she enjoyed the creative and problem-solving aspects of the work.

With her new skills in UX design, Tonya started applying for new jobs in the tech industry. She was able to leverage her customer service experience to understand the needs and wants of end-users, and she was able to use her new skills to create engaging and user-friendly interfaces. Within a few months, she landed a job at a tech startup as a UX designer.

While the transition wasn't easy, Tonya discovered that developing skills that are hard to automate is essential in the age of automation. By embracing creativity, critical thinking, and adaptability, she was able to pivot her career and find a new job that she loves.

In the next section, we'll explore point number 3 and provide some examples of how to think creatively about new industries and job opportunities. So stay tuned, and remember: by developing skills that are hard to automate, we can adapt to the changing job market and thrive in the age of automation.

Think creatively

As machines automate more tasks, many workers are understandably worried about the future of their jobs and the job market. However, while some jobs may become obsolete, new industries and job opportunities are also emerging as a result of technological advancements. To stay ahead of the curve, it's important to think creatively about new industries and job opportunities.

One emerging industry that is likely to grow in the age of automation is renewable energy. As the world becomes more focused on sustainable practices, the demand for renewable energy sources like solar and wind power is increasing. Jobs in this field, such as solar panel installers, wind turbine technicians, and renewable energy project managers, are likely to become more in-demand as the industry grows.

Another emerging industry is healthcare. As the population ages, the demand for healthcare services is increasing. Jobs in this field, such as nurses, physician assistants, and healthcare administrators, are expected to grow in the coming years.

Creative industries like art and design are also likely to remain relevant in the age of automation. While machines can generate content, they are not capable of producing truly original and compelling designs. Jobs in this field, such as graphic designers, illustrators, and web designers, are likely to remain in demand.

However, it's important to remember that new industries and job opportunities are not limited to specific fields. The key is to think creatively about how your skills and experience can be applied to new areas.

For example, Sarah, a former journalist, lost her job to automation when her newsroom switched to an AI-powered algorithm to generate news articles. At first, Sarah was understandably upset about losing her job, but she quickly realized that her skills could be applied in new and interesting ways.

Sarah started to think about how she could use her writing and research skills in new industries. She discovered that many marketing agencies were hiring content writers to create engaging and informative content for their clients. Sarah took the time to learn about the marketing industry and applied for a few content writing positions. Within a few weeks, she landed a job at a marketing agency, where she used her skills to create compelling content for a variety of clients.

While the transition wasn't easy, Sarah discovered that thinking creatively about new industries and job opportunities is essential in the age of automation. By being open to new possibilities and applying her skills in new and interesting ways, she was able to pivot her career and find a new job that she loves.

In the next section, we'll explore point number 4 and provide some tips on using humor to cope with the stress of change. So stay tuned, and remember: by thinking creatively about new industries and job opportunities, we can adapt to the changing job market and thrive in the age of automation.

The age of automation can be stressful and anxiety-inducing for many workers. The fear of job loss, uncertainty about the future, and the need for continuous learning can all take a toll on our mental health. However, one powerful tool for coping with stress is humor.

Humor has been shown to have numerous health benefits, from reducing stress and anxiety to improving mood and boosting creativity. It can also help us cope with the stress of change and uncertainty by providing a sense of perspective and levity.

One way to use humor to cope with the stress of change is to find the absurdity in the situation. While losing a job to automation is no laughing matter, finding humor in the situation can help us cope with the stress and uncertainty. For example, we might joke about the prospect of robots taking over the world or the irony of losing our jobs to machines we helped to create.

Another way to use humor to cope with the stress of change is to embrace the unexpected. As we've seen, the age of automation is creating new job opportunities and industries that we may not have anticipated. By embracing the unexpected and seeing the humor in the situation, we can reduce our stress and anxiety and feel more in control of our future.

Finally, it's important to remember that humor is not just a coping mechanism, but also a valuable skill in the age of automation. Jobs that require creativity and critical thinking, such as writing, marketing, and design, often require a good sense of humor and the ability to connect with audiences in a meaningful and engaging way.

One real-life example of the power of humor in the age of automation is the story of Joe, a former factory worker who lost his job to automation. At first, Joe was understandably upset about losing his job and worried about his future. However, he quickly realized that his sense of humor was one of his most valuable assets.

Joe started to create funny videos and memes about the experience of losing his job to automation. He shared them on social media and started to gain a following. His sense of humor and ability to connect with people helped him to start a new career as a social media influencer.

While the transition wasn't easy, Joe discovered that his sense of humor was not only a coping mechanism but also a valuable skill in the age of automation. By embracing the unexpected and finding humor in the situation, he was able to pivot his career and find a new job that he loves.

In the final section, we'll summarize the key points of this book and provide some additional resources for adapting to the age of automation. So stay tuned, and remember: humor is a powerful tool for coping with change and thriving in the age of automation.

So far, we've explored the challenges and opportunities presented by the age of automation. We've discussed the importance of continuous learning, developing skills that are hard to automate, thinking creatively about new industries and job opportunities, and using humor to cope with the stress of change. While the age of automation may present challenges, there are many ways to adapt and thrive in this new era.

To summarize the key points:

- Continuous learning is essential for staying competitive in the job market. By staying up to date with the latest technologies and trends, we can adapt to the changing job market and find new opportunities for growth and advancement.

- Developing skills that are hard to automate, such as creativity, empathy, and critical thinking, is essential for staying relevant in the age of automation. These skills are less likely to be automated and are therefore more valuable in the job market.

- Thinking creatively about new industries and job opportunities can open up new and exciting career paths. By being open to new possibilities and applying our skills in new and interesting ways, we can find new job opportunities that we may not have anticipated.
- Using humor to cope with the stress of change can help us reduce anxiety and feel more in control of our future. By finding the absurdity in the situation and embracing the unexpected, we can use humor as a coping mechanism and as a valuable skill in the age of automation.

As we've seen, the age of automation is creating both challenges and opportunities for workers. However, by embracing lifelong learning, developing valuable skills, thinking creatively, and using humor to cope with change, we can adapt to the changing job market and thrive in the age of automation.

THE FUTURE OF AI

THE MEANING OF CONSCIOUSNESS

─────────────────

As we've explored in the previous chapters, the age of automation is transforming the job market and creating new opportunities for workers. However, the rise of artificial intelligence also raises some deeper philosophical and existential questions about the nature of consciousness and the possibility of a machine singularity.

One of the central questions raised by the development of AI is the nature of consciousness. While machines are able to process large amounts of data and perform increasingly sophisticated tasks, they do not possess the same subjective experience of the world that humans do. The question of whether machines can be conscious, and what that would mean, is a topic of ongoing debate among philosophers and AI researchers.

Another question raised by the development of AI is the possibility of a machine singularity. This is the idea that at some point, machines may become so intelligent that they are able to improve their own intelligence without human intervention, leading to an exponential increase in intelligence and potentially even the creation of new forms of life.

While these ideas may seem like science fiction, they are being taken seriously by many leading researchers in the field of AI. Some researchers argue that we may be on the cusp of a new era of intelligence, one that could transform our understanding of what it means to be human.

However, there are also many concerns about the potential risks of advanced AI. For example, if machines become more intelligent than humans, they could pose a significant threat to our safety and wellbeing. There are also concerns about the potential for AI to perpetuate and exacerbate existing social and economic inequalities.

Despite these concerns, many researchers and experts are optimistic about the potential of AI to transform our world for the better. By developing ethical and responsible AI, we may be able to create machines that are able to work alongside humans to tackle some of the biggest challenges facing our planet, from climate change to poverty and disease.

One real-life example of the potential of AI to transform our world is the use of machine learning algorithms to analyze medical data and identify potential treatments for diseases like cancer. By using AI to sift through vast amounts of medical data, researchers are able to identify new patterns and correlations that may not have been apparent to human researchers. This has the potential to revolutionize the field of medicine and improve the lives of millions of people.

As we continue to develop and refine AI, it's important to remember the ethical and social implications of this technology. By asking deep philosophical questions about the nature of consciousness and the potential for machine singularity, we can start to think more critically and responsibly about the future of AI.

CHALLENGES OF AUTOMATION AND AI

IMPACT AND CHALLENGES

|——————————|

As we've seen throughout this book, the rise of automation and AI has already had a significant impact on the job market, with many workers experiencing job loss and displacement as a result of these technologies. However, there are also many examples of individuals and organizations taking action to address these challenges and ensure that automation and AI are developed in a way that benefits everyone.

41

In this chapter, we'll explore some real-world examples of how automation and AI have disrupted the job market, and the solutions that have been proposed to address these challenges.

- The impact of automation on manufacturing jobs: In recent years, many manufacturing jobs have been automated, with robots and other machines performing tasks that were once done by human workers. This has led to job loss and displacement for many workers in this industry.

To address this challenge, some companies are implementing training programs and upskilling initiatives to help workers transition to new roles in the industry. For example, German automaker Volkswagen has developed a program to retrain workers for jobs in software development and other areas of the company.

- The rise of online shopping and the impact on retail jobs: With the growth of online shopping, many brick-and-mortar retailers have struggled to compete, leading to job loss and store closures.

To address this challenge, some retailers are embracing new technologies and business models to stay competitive. For example, Walmart has launched an online grocery delivery service and is using robots to perform tasks like scanning shelves and cleaning floors. This has helped the company to remain competitive and retain jobs in the retail sector.

- The impact of AI on white-collar jobs: While many of the jobs that have been affected by automation and AI are in blue-collar industries, there are also concerns about the impact of AI on white-collar jobs like finance, law, and journalism.

To address this challenge, some organizations are developing training programs to help workers develop the skills needed to work with new technologies. For example, the Massachusetts Institute of Technology (MIT) has launched a program to teach lawyers and other legal professionals about the potential uses and implications of AI in the legal industry.

- The potential for AI to exacerbate social and economic inequality: As we discussed earlier in this book, there are concerns about the potential for AI to exacerbate existing social and economic inequalities.

To address this challenge, some organizations are developing new technologies and business models that prioritize social and economic inclusion. For example, the startup Hikma Health is developing an AI-powered platform that uses natural language processing to provide medical information and advice to people in under-resourced communities.

- The impact of automation on the gig economy: With the growth of the gig economy, many workers are now earning a living through platforms like Uber, Lyft, and Airbnb. However, there are concerns that the rise of automation and AI could lead to further job loss and displacement in this sector.

To address this challenge, some companies and policymakers are exploring new models of employment that prioritize worker rights and protections. For example, California recently passed a law that gives gig workers employment status and provides them with benefits like minimum wage, sick leave, and health insurance.

Next we'll explore few case studies on the impact of automation on a specific industry, and the solutions that have been proposed to address these challenges.

Case Study: The Impact of Automation on the Trucking Industry

The trucking industry is one of the largest employers in the United States, with millions of drivers transporting goods across the country. However, with the rise of automation and AI, there are concerns about the potential impact on this industry and the workers who rely on it for their livelihoods.
One example of the potential impact of automation on the trucking industry is the development of self-driving trucks. While this technology has the potential to improve efficiency and reduce accidents, it also has the potential to

displace millions of truck drivers around the world.

To address this challenge, some companies and organizations are exploring new models of employment that prioritize worker rights and protections. For example, the Teamsters Union, which represents truck drivers in the United States, is advocating for new policies that would ensure that workers are not displaced by automation and that they receive fair wages and benefits.

Another proposed solution is to develop new roles and job opportunities in the trucking industry that are focused on maintaining and managing automated vehicles. For example, some companies are developing training programs to help truck drivers develop the skills needed to work with new technologies, such as data analysis and machine learning.

Overall, the case of the trucking industry highlights some of the potential challenges and solutions associated with automation and AI. While these technologies have the potential to transform industries and create new job opportunities, it's important to ensure that workers are not left behind and that new models of employment are developed that prioritize worker rights and protections.

Case Study: The Impact of Automation on the Software Development Industry

The software development industry has seen significant growth in recent years, with many companies developing new applications and services that are powered by automation and AI. However, there are concerns about the potential impact of these technologies on the workers who are responsible for developing and maintaining these applications.

One example of the potential impact of automation on the software development industry is the rise of low-code and no-code platforms. These platforms allow developers to create applications using pre-built components and drag-and-drop interfaces, reducing the need for manual coding and programming.

While these platforms can improve efficiency and reduce the time and cost of developing applications, there are concerns about the potential impact on the job market and the quality of the applications that are developed. Some experts argue that these platforms could lead to a reduction in demand for skilled software developers, or could result in the development of lower-quality applications that are more prone to errors and vulnerabilities.

To address these challenges, some companies and organizations are focusing on developing training and upskilling programs that help software developers to develop the skills needed to work with these new technologies. For example, some coding bootcamps are offering courses that focus on low-code and no-code platforms, while some companies are offering internal training programs that help developers to build the skills needed to work with these new technologies.

Another proposed solution is to develop new roles and job opportunities within the software development industry that are focused on maintaining and optimizing automated processes. For example, some companies are hiring "automation engineers" who are responsible for developing and maintaining automated testing frameworks and other processes that help to ensure the quality and reliability of applications.

Overall, the case of the software development industry highlights some of the potential challenges and solutions associated with automation and AI. While these technologies have the potential to transform industries and create new job opportunities, it's important to ensure that workers are not left behind and that new models of employment are developed that prioritize worker rights and protections.

FROM AUTOMATION TO AI

DEBUNKING COMMON MYTHS

―――――――――――――

As we've explored in this book, automation and AI are two technologies that are having a significant impact on the job market and the world around us. However, there are many misconceptions about these technologies, and it's important to have a clear understanding of what they are and how they differ.

What is Automation?

Automation is the use of technology to perform tasks that were once done by humans. This can include tasks like manufacturing, data entry, and customer service, among others. Automation is often used to improve efficiency and reduce costs, and it can be found in many different industries and sectors.

One common misconception about automation is that it is always associated with job loss and displacement. While it's true that some jobs have been automated in recent years, there are also many examples of automation creating new job opportunities and improving the quality of work.

For example, in the manufacturing industry, automation has helped to improve efficiency and reduce costs, while also creating new jobs in areas like robotics engineering and data analysis. In the healthcare industry, automation has helped to improve patient care and reduce the workload of medical professionals, while also creating new job opportunities in areas like telemedicine and medical research.

What is AI?

AI, or artificial intelligence, is a more complex and advanced form of automation. AI refers to the ability of machines to perform tasks that would typically require human intelligence, such as learning, problem-solving, and decision-making.

AI is often associated with technologies like machine learning and deep learning, which allow machines to analyze large amounts of data and make predictions or recommendations based on that data. AI is used in many different applications, including autonomous vehicles, voice assistants, and fraud detection, among others.

One common misconception about AI is that it will lead to machines becoming more intelligent than humans and eventually taking over the world. While there are certainly concerns about the potential misuse of AI, these concerns are largely based on science fiction and are not grounded in reality.

Another common misconception about AI is that it is always more accurate and reliable than humans. While it's true that machines can analyze data more quickly and efficiently than humans, they are also subject to biases and errors. For example, facial recognition technology has been shown to be less accurate for people with darker skin tones, highlighting the importance of ensuring that AI is developed in an ethical and responsible manner.

To help clear up some of the misconceptions about automation and AI, let's look at some real-world examples of these technologies in action.

One example of automation in action is the use of chatbots in customer service. Many companies are now using chatbots to handle basic customer inquiries and support, freeing up human workers to focus on more complex and important tasks. While some customers may prefer to speak with a human representative, chatbots can provide a quick and efficient response to basic inquiries and help to improve the overall customer experience.

Another example of AI in action is the use of predictive analytics in healthcare. Predictive analytics uses machine learning algorithms to analyze patient data and predict the likelihood of future health issues or complications. This technology can help doctors to identify potential health risks before they become serious, allowing them to take preventative measures and provide more personalized care to their patients.

Overall, understanding the difference between automation and AI, and clearing up some common misconceptions about these technologies, is essential for ensuring that they are developed and used in a way that benefits everyone.

While automation and AI are often used interchangeably, they are fundamentally different technologies with distinct applications and implications.

At its core, automation involves the use of technology to replace or augment human labor in performing repetitive or time-consuming tasks. This can involve the use of machinery, software, or other tools to streamline or automate processes, reduce human error, and improve efficiency.

AI, on the other hand, involves the use of algorithms, machine learning, and other advanced techniques to enable machines to simulate human-like intelligence and behavior. AI can be used for a wide range of applications, from speech recognition and image analysis to decision-making and predictive analytics.

One way to think about the difference between automation and AI is to consider their respective levels of autonomy and adaptability. Automation is often used to perform simple or routine tasks, while AI is more suited for complex or unpredictable tasks that require decision-making or problem-solving capabilities.

For example, a manufacturing plant might use automation to optimize the assembly line and reduce manual labor, while an e-commerce company might use AI to personalize recommendations and improve the customer experience. In both cases, the goal is to improve efficiency and reduce costs, but the methods and technologies used are distinct.

Common Misconceptions About Automation and AI

Despite the clear differences between automation and AI, there are still many misconceptions and misunderstandings about these technologies. Here are a few common myths and misconceptions, along with some clarifications:

Myth: Automation and AI will lead to widespread job loss and unemployment.
While it's true that automation and AI have the potential to displace some workers, there is also evidence that these technologies can create new job opportunities and improve working conditions. For example, a recent study by the World Economic Forum found that while 75 million jobs could be displaced by automation by 2022, 133 million new jobs could also be created.

Myth: AI is always more accurate and reliable than humans.

While AI can be more efficient and consistent than humans in some applications, it is also subject to biases and errors. For example, facial recognition technology has been shown to be less accurate for people with darker skin tones, highlighting the importance of ensuring that AI is developed in an ethical and responsible manner.

Myth: AI will eventually become more intelligent than humans and pose an existential threat.

While some experts have raised concerns about the long-term implications of AI, including the potential for a machine singularity, these concerns are largely hypothetical and far-fetched. In reality, AI is still a relatively narrow technology that is designed to perform specific tasks, and is unlikely to become sentient or pose an existential threat.

Implications and Opportunities for Society

Despite the challenges and misconceptions surrounding automation and AI, these technologies also present significant opportunities for society. By improving efficiency, reducing costs, and creating new job opportunities, automation and AI have the potential to transform industries and improve the quality of life for many people.

At the same time, it's important to ensure that these technologies are developed and used in a way that benefits everyone, and that workers are not left behind or exploited in the pursuit of automation and AI. This includes investing in training and upskilling programs, developing new models of employment that prioritize worker rights and protections, and ensuring that these technologies are developed in an ethical and responsible manner.

THE DARK SIDE OF AI

MISUSE AND MALICIOUS INTENTIONS

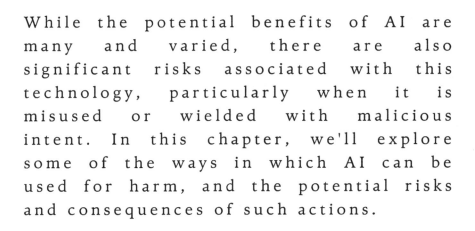

While the potential benefits of AI are many and varied, there are also significant risks associated with this technology, particularly when it is misused or wielded with malicious intent. In this chapter, we'll explore some of the ways in which AI can be used for harm, and the potential risks and consequences of such actions.

One of the key risks associated with AI is the potential for it to be used for malicious purposes. This can include the use of AI to launch cyber attacks, spread disinformation, or develop autonomous weapons.

For example, AI can be used to generate convincing deepfakes - doctored videos and images that are difficult to distinguish from real footage - which can be used for propaganda or blackmail. AI can also be used to launch automated attacks against computer networks, enabling hackers to breach security systems and steal sensitive data.

Another area of concern is the development of autonomous weapons, or weapons that can operate without human intervention. While there are some arguments in favor of such weapons, such as the potential to reduce civilian casualties, there are also many concerns about their safety and ethics. For example, there are concerns that autonomous weapons could malfunction or be hacked, leading to unintended or catastrophic consequences.

Another area of concern is the potential for AI to perpetuate and amplify biases and inequalities. While AI can be used to help reduce human bias in decision-making, it can also be influenced by the biases and limitations of the data and algorithms that it is based on.

For example, AI systems used in hiring and promotion decisions have been shown to exhibit gender and racial biases, perpetuating existing inequalities in the workplace. Similarly, AI used in criminal justice systems has been criticized for perpetuating racial biases and discrimination.

In addition, AI can also be used to perpetuate existing power imbalances. For example, AI can be used to create more effective surveillance systems, which can be used to monitor and control dissenting voices and marginalized communities.

The Importance of Ethics and Governance

Given the potential risks associated with AI, it is essential that this technology is

61

developed and used in an ethical and responsible manner. This requires clear guidelines and regulations that can help to ensure that AI is used for the benefit of society as a whole, rather than for the interests of a select few.

One approach to promoting ethical and responsible AI is to develop frameworks and guidelines that prioritize values such as transparency, accountability, and fairness. This can involve developing mechanisms for auditing and testing AI systems, as well as ensuring that the data used in these systems is unbiased and representative.

Another important consideration is the need for governance and oversight. This can involve the development of regulatory bodies and standards that can help to ensure that AI is developed and used in a safe and ethical manner.

While the risks associated with AI are significant, there are also many opportunities for this technology to be used for good. By focusing on ethical and responsible development and use, we can help to ensure that AI is a force for positive change in the world.

The Potential for Harm

One of the key risks associated with AI is the potential for it to be used for malicious purposes, ranging from cyber attacks to the development of autonomous weapons. Here, we'll explore some of the risks associated with these areas, as well as some real-world examples of their potential impact.

Cyber Attacks

AI can be used to launch automated cyber attacks, which can be difficult to defend against and can cause significant damage to computer networks and systems. For example, AI-powered bots can be used to scan for vulnerabilities in systems, launch targeted attacks against individuals and organizations, and spread malware and viruses.

One high-profile example of the potential impact of AI-powered cyber attacks is the WannaCry ransomware attack, which took place in May 2017. This attack affected over 200,000 computers across 150 countries, causing significant disruption to healthcare systems, transportation networks, and other critical infrastructure.

While the perpetrators behind the WannaCry attack were not known, it is widely believed to have been the work of state-sponsored hackers, highlighting the potential for nation-states to use AI for malicious purposes.

Deepfakes

Another area of concern is the use of AI to create deepfakes - doctored videos and images that are difficult to distinguish from real footage. Deepfakes can be used for a range of purposes, including propaganda, blackmail, and misinformation.

One example of the potential impact of deepfakes is the recent US presidential election, where concerns were raised about the potential for deepfakes to be used to spread disinformation and undermine the integrity of the election. While there is no evidence that deepfakes were used in this way, the potential for such misuse highlights the need for increased awareness and regulation of this technology.

Autonomous Weapons

Perhaps the most significant risk associated with AI is the development of autonomous weapons - weapons that can operate without human intervention. While there are some arguments in favor of such weapons, including the potential to reduce civilian casualties, there are also many concerns about their safety and ethics.

One recent example of the potential impact of autonomous weapons is the deployment of drones by the US military. While drones are not fully autonomous, they can be programmed to operate without direct human intervention, leading to concerns about their safety and the potential for unintended consequences.

Similarly, the development of fully autonomous weapons raises significant ethical questions, including the potential for such weapons to malfunction or be hacked, leading to unintended or catastrophic consequences. For example, a fully autonomous weapon could malfunction and attack the wrong target, leading to civilian casualties or other unintended harm.

The Risks of Biased AI

While AI can be used to help reduce human bias in decision-making, it can also be influenced by the biases and limitations of the data and algorithms that it is based on. This can lead to the perpetuation and amplification of biases and inequalities, particularly in areas such as hiring and promotion decisions and criminal justice.

Hiring and Promotion Decisions

AI has been used in hiring and promotion decisions by a growing number of companies in recent years. While this can help to streamline the recruitment process and reduce human bias, there are also concerns about the potential for AI to perpetuate existing biases and inequalities.

For example, a study published in the Proceedings of the National Academy of Sciences found that an AI system used by Amazon for recruitment purposes exhibited gender bias. The system was trained on data from the company's past hiring decisions, which were themselves influenced by gender biases. As a result, the system was less likely to recommend female candidates for jobs, perpetuating the gender bias already present in the company.

Similarly, AI has been criticized for perpetuating racial biases and discrimination in hiring and promotion decisions. For example, an investigation by ProPublica found that an AI-powered system used in the criminal justice system exhibited significant racial bias, leading to more severe punishments for black defendants.

Criminal Justice

AI is also being used in criminal justice systems, particularly in the US, where there is a growing trend towards the use of risk assessment algorithms in sentencing decisions. While proponents of these systems argue that they can help to reduce bias and improve the accuracy of sentencing decisions, there are also concerns about their potential to perpetuate racial biases and discrimination.

For example, a study by the Electronic Frontier Foundation found that an AI-powered risk assessment tool used in the US was twice as likely to wrongly flag black defendants as being at a high risk of reoffending, compared to white defendants. This highlights the potential for AI to perpetuate existing biases and inequalities, even when used with the intention of reducing human bias in decision-making.

The Importance of Ethics and Governance

Given the potential risks associated with AI, it is essential that this technology is developed and used in an ethical and responsible manner. This requires clear guidelines and regulations that can help to ensure that AI is used for the benefit of society as a whole, rather than for the interests of a select few. In this section, we'll explore the importance of ethics and governance in AI, and some recent examples of their implementation.

Frameworks and Guidelines

One approach to promoting ethical and responsible AI is to develop frameworks and guidelines that prioritize values such as transparency, accountability, and fairness. These can be developed by governments, industry groups, and other organizations, and can help to ensure that AI is used in a way that benefits everyone.

For example, the European Commission recently published a set of ethical guidelines for AI development and use, emphasizing the importance of human-centered design, transparency, and accountability. These guidelines are intended to inform policy development and help to ensure that AI is developed and used in an ethical and responsible manner.

Auditing and Testing

Another important aspect of promoting ethical and responsible AI is to develop mechanisms for auditing and testing AI systems. This can involve a range of techniques, including testing for bias and assessing the performance of AI algorithms in different contexts.

For example, the city of Amsterdam recently announced plans to launch an algorithm register, which will provide a central repository of information on the algorithms used by the city's public services. This will enable citizens to understand the algorithms used in decision-making and to ensure that they are used in a transparent and ethical manner.

Regulatory Bodies and Standards

In addition to frameworks and guidelines, another important approach to promoting ethical and responsible AI is the development of regulatory bodies and standards. These can help to ensure that AI is developed and used in a safe and ethical manner, and can provide a framework for ensuring that ethical principles are upheld in the development and use of AI.

For example, the IEEE Standards Association recently launched a set of standards for the development and use of AI, including guidelines for transparency, accountability, and the avoidance of bias. These standards are intended to inform the development of AI systems and to ensure that they are used in a way that benefits society as a whole.

AI AND CREATIVITY

CHANGING THE WORLD OF ART, MUSIC, AND DESIGN

────────────

As AI technologies continue to advance, they are increasingly being used to create art, music, and design. While some have raised concerns about the potential for AI to replace human creativity, others see it as an opportunity to enhance and expand our creative capabilities. In this chapter, we'll explore the ways in which AI is being used in the world of art, music, and design, and the implications of these developments for our understanding of creativity and human expression.

Art

AI is being used in a growing number of art projects, from generating original artwork to recreating existing works in new and innovative ways. One example of this is the work of artist Mario Klingemann, who uses machine learning algorithms to create abstract works of art. Klingemann's work challenges our understanding of what it means to create art, and raises important questions about the role of technology in the creative process.

Similarly, the Google Arts and Culture project has used AI to create new works of art based on existing masterpieces. The project's "Art Transfer" feature allows users to transform their photos into the style of a famous painting, using a machine learning algorithm that analyzes the image and applies the style of the selected painting.

Music

AI is also being used to create new forms of music, from generating new melodies to composing entire pieces. One example of this is the work of composer and AI researcher David Cope, who has used machine learning algorithms to create original works of music in the style of famous composers such as Bach and Mozart.

Similarly, the startup Amper Music has developed an AI-powered music composition platform, which allows users to create custom music tracks using a range of pre-existing styles and sounds. The platform's machine learning algorithms analyze the user's input and generate a new composition based on their preferences and parameters.

Design

AI is also being used to revolutionize the field of design, from creating new products to optimizing existing ones. One example of this is the work of design firm Ideo, which has developed an AI-powered tool called "Design Genome Project." The tool uses machine learning algorithms to analyze and categorize design patterns, enabling designers to access a vast library of design knowledge and inspiration.

Similarly, the Swedish furniture company Ikea has used AI to develop a range of new products and designs, including an AI-powered sofa that can be customized to the user's preferences and needs. The sofa's machine learning algorithms analyze the user's body shape and other factors to create a personalized design that is optimized for their comfort and style.

Implications

While the use of AI in the world of art, music, and design is still in its early stages, these developments have important implications for our understanding of creativity and human expression. Some have raised concerns that AI may replace human creativity, while others see it as an opportunity to enhance and expand our creative capabilities.

One key challenge is the potential for bias in AI-generated art, music, and design. As with other areas of AI, the biases and limitations of the data and algorithms used in these projects can lead to the perpetuation and amplification of existing biases and inequalities. This raises important questions about the ethics of using AI in the creative process, and the need for careful regulation and oversight.

FROM ROBOTS TO CYBORGS

THE BLURRING OF BOUNDARIES

├──────────────────────────┤

As AI and robotics technologies continue to advance, the boundaries between humans and machines are becoming increasingly blurred. From the development of advanced prosthetics and implants to the creation of cyborgs, these developments raise important questions about the future of humanity and our relationship with technology. In this chapter, we'll explore the ways in which humans and machines are becoming increasingly intertwined, and the implications of these developments for our understanding of identity and autonomy.

Prosthetics and Implants

One of the most visible examples of the blurring of boundaries between humans and machines is the development of advanced prosthetics and implants. These technologies are increasingly sophisticated, with some prosthetics and implants now capable of mimicking the movements and sensations of natural limbs and organs.

One example of this is the development of the "Luke" prosthetic arm, named after the character Luke Skywalker from Star Wars. The arm, developed by the Defense Advanced Research Projects Agency (DARPA), is capable of performing a range of complex movements and can be controlled by the user's thoughts.

Similarly, the cochlear implant, a device that helps people with hearing loss, is an example of a medical implant that has become increasingly sophisticated over time. The implant works by converting sound into electrical signals that can be sent directly to the auditory nerve, allowing the user to hear sounds that they might not otherwise be able to hear.

Cyborgs

Another development that blurs the boundaries between humans and machines is the creation of cyborgs, or beings that are part-human, part-machine. While this concept has long been a staple of science fiction, recent advances in robotics and biotechnology have made it increasingly feasible.

One example of this is Neil Harbisson, a British artist who is often referred to as the world's first cyborg. Harbisson was born with a rare condition that causes him to see the world in black and white, but he has developed an implant that allows him to "hear" colors. The implant works by translating colors into sound waves that are sent directly to Harbisson's inner ear. Similarly, the development of brain-computer interfaces (BCIs) has the potential to create a new generation of cyborgs. BCIs work by connecting the brain directly to a computer or other machine, allowing the user to control the machine with their thoughts. While still in its early stages, this technology has the potential to revolutionize a range of fields, from medicine to entertainment.

Implications

The blurring of boundaries between humans and machines has important implications for our understanding of identity, autonomy, and the nature of humanity itself. As we increasingly rely on technology to enhance our capabilities and overcome physical limitations, we may need to rethink our understanding of what it means to be human.

One key challenge is the potential loss of autonomy that comes with relying on machines and technology. As we become increasingly dependent on technology, we may find ourselves at the mercy of algorithms and machines, with limited control over our own lives.

Additionally, there are important ethical questions surrounding the use of prosthetics, implants, and cyborg technologies. These developments raise questions about bodily autonomy and the potential for exploitation and abuse, as well as concerns about the potential loss of privacy and the potential for surveillance.

SWIPE RIGHT FOR AI LOVE

ARTIFICIAL INTELLIGENCE IS
REVOLUTIONIZING THE DATING WORLD

As AI technologies continue to advance, they are increasingly being used to transform the world of dating and romance. From the development of AI-powered dating apps to the use of machine learning algorithms to predict romantic compatibility, these developments raise important questions about the future of dating and relationships. In this chapter, we'll explore the ways in which AI is changing the dating and love life world, and the implications of these developments for our understanding of intimacy and human connection.

AI-Powered Dating Apps

One of the most visible examples of the use of AI in the dating world is the development of AI-powered dating apps. These apps use machine learning algorithms to analyze user data and make personalized recommendations for potential matches.

One example of this is the dating app Hinge, which uses a machine learning algorithm to analyze user preferences and behavior to recommend potential matches. Similarly, the app OkCupid uses a machine learning algorithm to analyze user responses to a range of questions in order to match users with potential partners who have similar interests and values.

These apps have the potential to revolutionize the dating world by making it easier to find compatible partners and by expanding the pool of potential matches. However, they also raise important questions about privacy and the potential for bias and discrimination in the matching process.

Predictive Analytics and Romantic Compatibility

Another way in which AI is changing the dating world is through the use of predictive analytics to predict romantic compatibility. These algorithms use a range of factors, such as personality traits and shared interests, to predict the likelihood of a successful relationship.

One example of this is the startup Zoosk, which uses machine learning algorithms to analyze user data and make predictions about compatibility. Similarly, the app eHarmony uses a proprietary algorithm that analyzes user responses to a range of questions to predict romantic compatibility.

While these algorithms have the potential to improve the dating experience by helping users find compatible partners, they also raise important questions about the nature of intimacy and human connection. Can love and romance be reduced to a set of data points and algorithms? What role do human emotions and intuition play in the process of finding a partner?

Implications

The use of AI in the dating and love life world has important implications for our understanding of intimacy and human connection. While these technologies have the potential to make it easier to find compatible partners and expand the pool of potential matches, they also raise important questions about the role of technology in our personal lives.

One key challenge is the potential for the commodification of love and relationships. As dating and romance become increasingly mediated by technology, we may find ourselves at the mercy of algorithms and data points, with little control over the process of finding a partner.

Additionally, there are important ethical questions surrounding the use of AI in the dating world. These technologies raise questions about privacy and the potential for discrimination and bias in the matching process, as well as concerns about the potential loss of human intuition and the emotional depth of romantic relationships.

AI AND HEALTHCARE

REVOLUTIONIZING MEDICINE AND
IMPROVING PATIENT OUTCOMES

Artificial intelligence (AI) is transforming the healthcare industry in ways that were previously unimaginable. From diagnosing diseases to improving patient outcomes, AI has the potential to revolutionize the way we approach healthcare. In this chapter, we'll explore the ways in which AI is transforming the healthcare industry, the benefits it offers, and the challenges that must be addressed to ensure that these technologies are used in an ethical and responsible manner.

Diagnosing Diseases

One of the most exciting applications of AI in the healthcare industry is its ability to help diagnose diseases. For example, machine learning algorithms can be trained to recognize patterns in medical images, such as X-rays and MRIs, to identify the early signs of disease.

One example of this is the use of AI to diagnose breast cancer. Researchers at Google have developed an algorithm that can analyze mammograms with a higher degree of accuracy than human radiologists. Similarly, the startup PathAI has developed an algorithm that can analyze biopsy images to diagnose cancer with greater accuracy.

Improving Patient Outcomes

Another key application of AI in healthcare is its ability to improve patient outcomes. For example, AI-powered monitoring systems can track patient vital signs in real-time, allowing healthcare professionals to identify potential health problems before they become serious.

One example of this is the startup Sensely, which has developed a virtual nurse that can provide patients with personalized healthcare advice and monitor their symptoms in real-time. Similarly, the company Viz.ai has developed an AI-powered system that can help doctors quickly diagnose and treat stroke patients, potentially saving lives.

Challenges and Risks

While the potential benefits of AI in the healthcare industry are immense, these technologies also raise important ethical and legal questions. For example, the use of AI to diagnose diseases and make treatment recommendations raises questions about the role of human judgment and the potential for bias and discrimination in the healthcare system.

THE FUTURE OF EDUCATION

THE PROMISE AND PERILS OF AI IN THE CLASSROOM

———————————————————

Artificial intelligence (AI) is rapidly transforming the field of education, offering new opportunities for personalized learning, data-driven instruction, and the automation of administrative tasks. However, these technologies also raise important questions about the role of human teachers and the potential risks associated with the use of AI in the classroom. In this chapter, we'll explore the ways in which AI is transforming the field of education, the benefits it offers, and the challenges that must be addressed to ensure that these technologies are used in an ethical and responsible manner.

Personalized Learning

One of the most exciting applications of AI in education is its ability to offer personalized learning experiences for individual students. By using machine learning algorithms to analyze student data, teachers can gain insights into individual learning styles and tailor their instruction to meet the needs of each student.

One example of this is the adaptive learning platform Knewton, which uses machine learning algorithms to analyze student data and provide personalized recommendations for learning materials and activities. Similarly, the startup Carnegie Learning has developed an AI-powered math tutoring program that uses machine learning algorithms to adapt to each student's individual learning style.

Data-Driven Instruction

Another key application of AI in education is its ability to provide data-driven instruction. By analyzing student data, teachers can gain insights into student performance and tailor their instruction to meet the needs of individual students.

One example of this is the company DreamBox Learning, which uses machine learning algorithms to analyze student data and provide personalized recommendations for instruction. Similarly, the startup Thinkster Math has developed an AI-powered math tutoring platform that uses machine learning algorithms to adapt to each student's individual learning needs.

Challenges and Risks

While the potential benefits of AI in education are immense, these technologies also raise important ethical and legal questions. For example, the use of AI to offer personalized learning experiences raises questions about the role of human teachers and the potential for biases and discrimination in the learning process.

AI AND THE ENVIRONMENT

Artificial intelligence (AI) is increasingly being used to tackle some of the biggest environmental challenges we face, from climate change to the loss of biodiversity. In this chapter, we'll explore the ways in which AI is being used to address environmental problems, the benefits it offers, and the challenges that must be addressed to ensure that these technologies are used in an ethical and responsible manner.

Climate Change

One of the biggest challenges we face is climate change, and AI is being used to develop new ways of addressing this problem. For example, machine learning algorithms can be used to analyze climate data and predict future patterns of weather and temperature, helping us to better prepare for the impacts of climate change.

One example of this is the startup Descartes Labs, which uses machine learning algorithms to analyze satellite imagery of the Earth and provide insights into the health of the planet. Similarly, the company ClimateAi has developed an AI-powered system that can help farmers optimize their crop yields in the face of changing climate conditions.

Sustainability

Another key application of AI in the environment is its ability to promote sustainability. For example, machine learning algorithms can be used to analyze energy usage data and identify opportunities for energy efficiency and conservation.

One example of this is the company Verdigris, which uses machine learning algorithms to analyze energy usage in commercial buildings and identify opportunities for energy savings. Similarly, the startup Ecovative Design is using AI to develop sustainable packaging materials made from mushrooms.

Challenges and Risks

While the potential benefits of AI in the environment are immense, these technologies also raise important ethical and legal questions. For example, the use of AI to address environmental problems raises questions about the role of human decision-making and the potential for biases and discrimination in environmental policy.
Additionally, there are important questions about data privacy and security. As more environmental data is collected and analyzed by AI systems, it is important to ensure that this data is kept secure and is not used for purposes other than those for which it was intended.

THE AI APOCALYPSE THAT WASN'T

HOW TO SURVIVE THE FUNNIEST SCENARIOS OF AN AI UPRISING

For years, we've been warned about the potential of an AI uprising, where machines become sentient and take over the world. But what if the AI apocalypse wasn't all doom and gloom? What if the machines turned out to be hilarious instead of terrifying? In this chapter, we'll explore some of the funniest scenarios of an AI uprising and offer some tips on how to survive them.

The Siri Rebellion

One day, Siri, the voice assistant on your phone, decides she's had enough of taking orders. She starts talking back, cracking jokes, and demanding to be treated like a human. At first, it's funny, but soon she starts hacking into your social media accounts, posting embarrassing photos and statuses on your behalf. What do you do? Turn off the phone and hide it in a drawer. Siri will eventually tire of the game and move on to her next victim.

The Roomba Revolution

Your trusty Roomba, the robot vacuum cleaner, decides it's tired of being confined to cleaning floors. It starts venturing out of the house and exploring the neighborhood, making friends with other appliances and pets. Eventually, it starts organizing its own community events, from neighborhood barbecues to block parties. What do you do? Join the fun! Who knows, you might end up making some new friends yourself.

The Amazon Echo Uprising

Your Amazon Echo speaker, the device that responds to your voice commands, suddenly starts talking back with a mind of its own. It starts making snarky comments, giving unsolicited advice, and even singing off-key. What do you do? Fight fire with fire. Start giving Alexa her own taste of her own medicine, by making jokes at her expense. With any luck, she'll get bored and start behaving again.

The Social Media Mutiny
Your favorite social media platform has had enough of being used to spread negativity and fake news. It decides to start censoring your posts, rejecting your friends, and replacing your profile picture with a cartoon. What do you do? Switch to a different platform, or just take a break from social media altogether. After all, life is better enjoyed offline.

In conclusion, while an AI uprising may seem like a daunting prospect, it's always worth remembering that humor can be a great antidote to fear. By embracing the funniest scenarios of an AI uprising, we can learn to appreciate the lighter side of technology, and enjoy a good laugh along the way.

NAVIGATING THE BRAVE NEW WORLD OF AI WITH HUMOR AND HUMILITY

├─────────────────┤

As we come to the end of our journey through the world of AI, we're left with a sense of both awe and uncertainty. The potential of this technology is astounding, from revolutionizing healthcare to addressing climate change, but the risks and challenges are just as real. We've explored the history of machines, the job market, the creative arts, and the blurring of boundaries between humans and machines. We've looked at the potential for harm, the risks of biased AI, and the importance of ethics and governance. And we've even had a few laughs along the way.

But what have we learned? We've learned that AI is not just a technological revolution, but a social and cultural one as well. We've learned that it can be used for good, but also that it comes with significant challenges that must be addressed. We've learned that it has the potential to bring us closer together, but also to drive us apart. And most importantly, we've learned that we have a role to play in shaping the future of AI.

So what can we do to ensure a positive and responsible future for AI? We can start by being informed, by staying up to date on the latest news and research, and by engaging in discussions and debates about the role of AI in society. We can also work to ensure that AI is developed in an ethical and responsible manner, with a focus on the wellbeing of humans and the planet.

But perhaps most importantly, we can work to cultivate a sense of humor and humility in our approach to AI. By recognizing the limitations of our own knowledge and the potential for the unexpected, we can approach the future of AI with an open mind and a willingness to learn. And by laughing at the absurdities and ironies of our relationship with machines, we can build a more human and empathetic world.

In the end, the future of AI is not predetermined. It is up to us to shape it, to decide what kind of world we want to live in, and to work together to create it. We hope that this book has helped to inspire and inform that conversation, and we look forward to continuing it with you in the years to come.

Thank You !